Beauty *from* Ashes

Finding yourself in and with God

A 21-day devotional to fortify your soul and facilitate intimacy with God.

Kerry Ann Richie Wilkinson

Beauty from Ashes. Finding yourself in and with God.
Copyright © 2021. Kerry Ann Richie Wilkinson

Published by:

Unless otherwise stated, Scripture quotations marked KJV are from the Holy Bible, King James Version (Authorized Version). First published in 1611. Quoted from the KJV Classic Reference Bible, Copyright 1983, by The Zondervan Corporation.

ISAIAH 61:1-3

1. The spirit of the Lord God is upon me; because the Lord hath anointed me to preach good tidings unto the meek; He had sent me to bind up the broken hearted, to proclaim liberty to the captives, and the opening of the prison to them that are bound.

2. To proclaim the acceptable year of the Lord, and the day of vengeance of our God; to comfort all that mourn;

3. To appoint unto them that mourn in Zion, to give unto them Beauty for Ashes, the oil of joy for mourning, the garment of praise for the spirit of heaviness; that they might be called trees of righteousness, the planting of the Lord, that he might be glorified.

Dedication

This book is dedicated to my grandmother Selona Wallace. It is a tangible evidence of the righteous and holy life that she lived that I now replicate.

Mommy, your love for Jesus was immeasurable. I now fathom your love for Him and your spiritual walk. You were full of glee. I couldn't understand then but now that I am consumed with the *Beauty* of Jesus and have been lifted from the *Ashes*. I can discern now that you were exhibiting the fruits of the Spirit.

May your sweet soul rest in peace. And may we meet again in Glory.

Acknowledgement

I want to first thank God my Father for this encounter. I thank Him for choosing me to be a vessel and allocating me with wisdom, knowledge and understanding by revealing who He is and who I am. With this enlightenment, I can effectively impart and share such great discovery with you.

It would be remiss of me if I did not mention and highlight my grandparents Selona and Cyril Wallace (deceased). My grandmother (mommy) who was an evangelist/prophet, instilled Biblical morals in me as a way of life. Now that I am old, I have not departed from it.

To my husband Jason Wilkinson, thank you for always being there for me. Sending me to my "prayer room" when it was time required for bed. You had no issues of my late-night writings.

I must acknowledge Pastor Ann Taylor. She was very instrumental in developing and managing my prophetic abilities. I attended her "School for Prophets" in North Carolina. Even though they are 4 hours away in distance, they accommodated and welcomed me with open arms. Your love, kindness and gentleness towards me helped me to see Jesus a little clearer. My "uniqueness was truly celebrated" as your vison states.

To Minister Suzette Lewis, thank you. You saw the calling of God on my life through my Facebook posts and kept nudging me to surrender my life to God. When I had my divine encounter you were the first person I called, all the way in Jamaica. You were also the first person to invite me to speak at a church and for that vote of confidence, I am grateful.

To my Editor Hilette Virgo. Even though many years have passed for our college days you didn't hesitate to help me "Tap into my Great-Nest" and usher me to my GREATNESS.

To my spiritual father Bishop Raymond Bowers in Jamaica. Thank you for training me . Having so many surpirse speaking engagements in one month made me feel like I was in a well needed spiritual boot camp and I appreciate it. You helped to develop my character. I really saw how you believed in my spiritual abilities, and this allowed me to be more accepting of the will of God in my life.

To all those who have encouraged me by watching my Facebook lives or offered support in any other way, I thank you. The warm welcome propels me to keep going. I appreciate you.

Thank you.

Table of Contents

Dedication..iv

Acknowledgement...v

Introduction...1

Prologue...4

Identity

Day 1
Come Just as You Are...10

Day 2
Conceptualized Before Conception.........................14

Day 3
Who are you really?...16

Day 4
God is Our Manufacturer.......................................19

Day 5
What is in a Name?...21

Day 6
What Anointing do you Operate Under?.................24

Day 7
It is Over for the Devil..27

Giftings

Day 8

Knock Knock…Who is there? Your calling.................31

Day 9

The Gift of Anointing.................................34

Day 10

Gifts and Purpose Revealed...........................36

Day 11

Gifts Developed: Hone your Skills....................39

Day 12

It is Your Season....................................42

Day 13

What is Your Mission?................................45

Day 14

Renouncing Self.....................................48

Worship

Day 15

Praise is Taught, Worship is Sought..................52

Day 16

Fasting Feeds the Soul..............................55

Day 17

Erecting the Altar..58

Day 18

You are Going to be Tested...61

Day 19

Don't Treat Your Bible like Junk Mail........................64

Day 20

Rise and worship: Just Do It!......................................67

Day 21

The Blessings of Music in Worship.............................69

Epilogue

Worshipping with Angels...73

About the Author...76

Introduction

The steps of a good man are ordered by the Lord:
and he delighteth in his way. (Psalm 37:23)

I am just reminiscing and grasping the fact that I am writing a devotional. Who would have thought? I am even more shocked that anyone would want me to be their leader. Even greater wonder is the fact that God would use someone like me. I considered myself the last person that God would use in this manner. I have cheated, lusted, lied, cursed and done many things that have brought dishonor to God.

I have not been the most outstanding citizen of society, but God! He came into my life and dismantled me then put me back together. God realigned me to the plans and purpose that He originally had for my life.

I was so lost losing my grandmother who raised me, then I lost my grandfather nine months later. I came to the United States on an academic scholarship three months after; away from friends and family with whom

I needed to share my grief. I think that is where my glue melted, and my seams came apart. I suffered with abandonment issues for years, attaching myself to people who meant me no good, but I stayed because I did not want to feel lonely and be seen as an outcast.

My grandmother loved me with everything in her and I knew it. When that love died, when that love disappeared, I knew no other love (Tears are falling down my eyes as I write this). This devotional is causing me to unearth all the pain and suffering I have endured. I was so upset with God. Why would he leave me like a chaff which the wind 'driveth' away? Why had he forsaken me? Broken relationships, broken friendships, heartbreaks by the ton– left right and center.

It wasn't until now that I realized that all that hurt, and pain was shaping me and molding me into who I am supposed to be. It was what took me back to Christ, Jehovah Rapha, my healer, to heal my heart. God hates when we hurt. As a matter of fact, God hurts when we hurt. He is quite familiar with our trials. He too was misrepresented, misunderstood, betrayed by close companions and forsaken by His friends. He was forced to carry his own cross to be crucified and then mocked by onlookers.

In lieu of all that, my only regret is that I was not saved sooner. The love, joy and peace that now exist inside me, flows like a river. I cannot explain or comprehend it. Sometimes I wish I could bottle it up and share it, but you can access this fountain of love all for yourself. I am a living testimony that God will turn your ashes to beauty if you let Him. This is my story, and it can be yours too: God will give you *Beauty from Ashes*.

Prologue

As a cosmetologist, I have had the opportunity to offer my expertise in beauty care and enhancement for ladies of all ages, stages, class and socio-economic background. Most often than not, no matter how exceptionally beautiful I regard my clients, they seem to be fixated on the imperfections and flaws in their natural image.

Even though they come to me for enhancement, in my eyes, they are perfect; but through their own mirror, they see mostly flaws and imperfections. What I deem as unique, they see as undesirable features. It is the same with God our Savior. He sees beyond the flaws and defects that sin has imposed upon His perfect creation.

I myself have been tarnished from birth. I have suffered mental handicap trying to fit the "perfect" mold that society dictates for us. This narrative has crippled the ability for me to emit the true essence of my existence for years. It was when I came to know and establish a relationship with God that I was able to rise from the insecurities that were triggered by my social environment. This is when I came to the realization that the world's view of perfection is a deception that was created by the enemy.

With the influence of social media, standards, morals, discipline and right doing have declined considerably. The weight and significance of our values have diminished to the press of a "like" and/or "follow" button, where the most outrageous and immoral conduct and images are being highlighted and are more likely to go viral, while "righteous" and uplifting contents are left in the dust.

Our minds and perceptions are then obscured with deception and we become less capable of discerning facts from fiction. If we cannot meet up to the standard of beauty that is showcased in the media, we regard ourselves as ugly, flawed and tarnished. We no longer see ourselves as the beautiful creatures God desires us to be (Genesis 1:27) and lose sight of the fact that we are fearfully and wonderfully made (Psalm 139:14).

God's intention was for us to maintain the perfectly pure and flawless image that He formed and fashioned Adam and Eve. Then sin interrupted the ideal and the succeeding generations degenerated, however, Jesus came and gave us the opportunity to be restored, to reclaim His beauty and to rise from the ashes through His precious blood.

If we could see ourselves from God's point of view, we would see so much more value, worth and beauty. He esteems us highly and has great plans and purposes for us as declared in Jeremiah 29:11. However, we must subject our self to Him and allow Him to give us a complete makeover.

"Ashes" is a powdery residue left after the burning of a substance. The remains of something destroyed or the remains of a human body after cremation. This suggests destruction or desecration of an entity through fire. We then can assume appropriately that something that was once whole was broken down and consumed and condensed into small particles called ashes.

Ashes, according to the definition presented in the Merriam-Webster Dictionary, is something that symbolizes grief, repentance or humiliation. The solid residue left when combustible material is thoroughly burnt or is oxidized by chemical. Ashes is a reminder of death. It is a symbol of sorrow for our sins. "You are dust and dust you will return..." Genesis 3:19

Oftentimes we read of persons in the Bible who would use sackcloth and ashes to publicly express their sorrow or regret of having done something wrong. Tamar is one such person mentioned in 2 Samuel 13:19 after her half-brother Amnon took advantage of her: "put ashes on her head and rent her garment of divers colors that was on her and laid her hand on her head and went on crying."

It is during our ash-like state or place of repentance that God desires to dwell in us. It is when we come to the end of ourselves that the Lord renews us into what He desires.

When we come to the end of ourself, after being used, abused, battered, experience burnout, stress, depression and scars from all the cares of life, God then comes in and redeems, reshapes, regenerates, reignites, restore, re-edify and reforms us from our lowest state of being then purifies and furnishes us into a brand new creation. He generates a new formula from or residue, a 'new you' chemistry and formulates a stronger potion of love, laughter and light-heartedness within us. He allows us to rise from the ashes and exude the true beauty that shines from within.

This book was birthed out of a 21 day fast, hence a 21-day devotional. I garnered a deeper connection with God during this time and was inspired to share my experiences to assist you in cultivating a Christlike lifestyle.

I uncovered the basis of the doubt and fear we all develop overtime, and I found the antidote, GOD. Many walk around like lost sheep because they do not know that their true purpose and identity is in Christ.

In this book I explored and highlighted three themes that are critical to our Christian walk: Identity, Giftings and Worship. I have subdivided the topics into bite size, digestible portions so that you can take small steps to initiate a more intimate relationship with our Savior.

I hope this book will help remove the scales from your eyes as they fell from mine. My hope is that it fortifies your weary soul.

At the end of the 21 days, I hope you find the joy and peace that surpasses all understanding. I implore you to find and establish your *Identity* in Christ, discover your purpose and *Giftings* and strive to live a life of *Worship* and adulation. No matter what fiery trials you have suffered, no matter how burnt and disfigured you may be emotionally and spiritually, you can be a true *Beauty* that rose from the *Ashes*.

Identity

Identity is the distinguishing character or personality of an individual. Individuality is the relation established by psychological identification. In other words, it is what defines us. Our identity tells who we are.

As Christians, it is critical that we establish our identity and discover our true beauty in Christ. For the next seven days we will explore how we can establish our identity in Christ.

Day 1

Come Just as You Are

In the beginning God Created the heaven and the earth. (Genesis 1:1)

Have you ever wondered what is the true meaning of life? or what is your life's purpose? Is this just it?

Have you ever heard people speak of 'manifesting' and referring to the 'Universe' as a divine being? Have you ever yielded to disbelief wondering if there is a God? or wondered if there is an after-life? If so, how can you know for certain? I myself have pondered on these things.

I have found some very convincing ideologies and have researched a few theories with the hope of finding fulfillment, but it was not until I truly found Christ and had a life-changing encounter with God that I made peace with my wondering thoughts. This is when I fully recognized God's true existence as a Supreme Being- the one who controls and created the universe.

Many of us were raised in the world and were socialized to do worldly things. many were not taught and instilled with Christian principles. We just grew up and fell in line with the masses.

We lived our lives as we were taught– school, job, family. In the wake of our worldly upbringing, it was not difficult for us to fall prey to the debasing lifestyle of fornication, partying, drug abuse and indulging in all the pleasures of life.

Others were taught about church or "dragged" to church, but how many remained in that upbringing? It is usually later in life that many revert to the path where they remember Jesus. Sadly, many had the intention of returning or making it right, thinking they had time but missed the opportunity to safeguard their soul's salvation, while others struggle daily with the lies of the enemy, wanting to find God but do not know how to.

In life we are faced with many decisions. One critical choice is to decide whether we are on the side of darkness or on God's side. We are either in sin or living a Christian life. We are either enjoying the fruits of the flesh or bearing spiritual fruits. We are either living for Satan or living for God. There is no middle ground or in between.

I use to think that if I lived my life as an outstanding citizen of society it would be well. I was safe as a "good" person. But not so. We don't know that we are lost until we are found. We do not know that we are blind until the Lord removes the scales from your eyes and enlighten our darkness with His truth.

I wanted to share that so you can understand that you might be living the way you know, the way you were taught, but if it is not a pure Christian life, it is not the correct way.

When God called me and I answered, He gave me my spiritual gifts. My eyes were opened. For the first time, I felt like I was really me; I truly understood who I was and whom I was made to be. That is when I was able to walk in my purpose and calling.

I did not have to fix myself and come to Him. He accepted me just as I was and then He started His work of renewal. When God renews, cleanse and gives you a new heart with a different pair of eyes and vision, your understanding of Him begins to get clearer. You look back on all those years and realize that you were going the wrong way. That is the reason God speaks about a renewing of the mind in Romans 12:2 *And be not conformed to this world: but be ye transformed by the re-*

newing of your mind, that ye may prove what is that good, and acceptable, and perfect, will of God.

Deep intimacy with God derives from one most broken self. It is in this vulnerable moment of submission that we give up our control of our life and surrender completely to Him.

This is an opportune time to surrender our lives to God. This is when we should be eager to forfeit our plans and pursuit of our will. This is when we should take a deeper gander into knowing God. This is when we hope that the man named Jesus will demonstrate His restorative power in you. He is calling you today to come just as you are!

Prayer: God, I want to know who I am in You. Please reveal yourself to me. Give me wisdom, knowledge and understanding of your Word and assist me in applying it to my life. Thank you for dying on the cross for me. Help me to make you proud. In Jesus' Name. Amen.

Beauty, rise from the ashes and come just as you are!

Day 2

Conceptualized Before Conception

And God said, Let us make man in our image, after our likeness: ...So God created man in his own image, in the image of God created he him; male and female created he them. (Genesis 1:26-27).

I remember one morning I woke up and was a little disheartened by rumors that I heard about myself. I was just getting into my gifting and was a little insecure and hurt about the comments made. However, I heard the Lord said, "you were conceptualized before conception".

He was reminding me, as my Creator that he took the time out to form and develop me. Every intricate detail, He thought of. Hence, it did not matter how others perceived me, what mattered was that God held me in remarkably high esteem and His plans for me were greater than what anyone thought or said about me.

You are also precious to Him. God was pleased with His creation in Genesis 31 as He saw that everything that he had made, and behold, it was incredibly good.

We possess the identity of Christ when we are in Christ. We have been curated for His purpose and He has given us His characteristics. Therefore, we should not take refuge or solace in the false identity that men try to establish for us.

The way you think about yourself, the way you are viewed by the world and the characteristics that defines you are your identity. Every single idiosyncrasy, every decision, every thought reflects who you are. Therefore, it is important that we fix our eyes on Christ so that we may act accordingly and be our true divine self.

Prayer: God my Creator, thank you for creating me in your image. I am your workmanship. Help me to walk in the path and purpose that your desire of me. Empty me of my own thoughts and ideas and fill me with You. You are all that matters. I love you. In Jesus' Name. Amen

Beauty, you were conceptualized before you were conceived. Rise from the ashes!

15

Day 3

Who are you really?

Before I formed thee in the belly I knew thee; and before, thou camest forth out of the womb, and I ordained thee a prophet unto the nations (Jeremiah 1:5)

Our identity does not find us later in life. Our defined purpose was birthed with us. For some, it was initially apparent, but for most, it is unearthed overtime. However, it is a misconception that we become all that we are. Who we are at the core was already interwoven in our DNA in our hair follicles, fingerprints, in our sweat glands, our tear ducts, our organs, our skin, our overall biological development when we were conceived, and our potentials are inexhaustible.

Usually, we associate or identify our calling by the role that we play in each other's lives like a mom or a dad or a brother or sister or a wife or by our profession. We are not our career or relationship. We are not our marriage.

There is much more to us than that. Our personality was carefully planned and deposited in our core being and only Creator God has a complete understanding of who we really are.

Jeremiah was uncertain of himself and thought he was inadequate to the calling that God had on his life, but God reminded Jeremiah that He called him even before he was formed in his mother's womb and that He knew Jeremiah. He had already sanctified Jeremiah and equipped him for his calling. So even though Jeremiah was young, God was letting Jeremiah know that he was already who he was supposed to be in Him. He was created to be a Prophet to the nations even before he was conceived.

The answer to who we are can only be found in the One who created us. He has the blueprint for our lives. He is waiting on us to open our hearts to establish our identity in Him.

Prayer: God, I want to live a purposeful life. Reveal your plans and purpose for my life. I want to manifest my full potential. You said in 1 Corinthians 2:9 that eyes have not seen or ears heard or even entered into the hearts of man the things which you have prepared for me. That is the level I want to live my life for you. Help me to excel in your glory. In Jesus' Name. Amen.

Beauty, rise from the ashes and establish your identity in the one who formed and fashioned you.

Day 4

God is Our Manufacturer

For thou hast possessed my reins: Thou hast covered me in my mother's womb. (Psalms 139:13)

One day while conducting Bible Study, I was explaining to my audience how God sees us and suddenly the Holy Spirit took over. It was like I had an epiphany. The Revelation came to me in a technical manner and the Spirit directed me on how to break it down in bite size pieces so that they could fully grasp the concept. The Holy Spirit said that God is our manufacturer. We are His creation. There is no prototype to us. In the same manner that we buy a product, whether it is kitchen appliances, tools, makeup or furniture, it all comes with an instruction manual.

Sometimes the product is defective and we must return it to the original Manufacturer. Sometimes a special tool or product is needed to remedy the problem and only the developer of the product can provide such devices. It is the same for us. God as manufacturer is the only one who knows how to fix us.

There are also times when products are being recalled or have a manufacturer's defect. However, in God there is no such thing. God docs not makc mistakcs.

There are times when we are encumbered with the trap of the enemy and become defective. We are hurled about by the fears, despair, betrayal, disappointments, anxiety, depression and mourning. However, it is in this state of sorrow and hopelessness that God takes pleasure in fixing us.

He is the only one who is equipped to fix our hearts. To exchange our ashes for beauty.

Prayer: God, please forgive me for not seeing my true worth and value in you. I Thank you for your perfect design. Mold me and make me; use me as an instrument of Thine. Let me realize that I have been uniquely packaged. In Jesus name. Amen

Beauty, your Manufacturer made you in His perfect image, rise from the ashes and establish your identity in Him!

Day 5

What is in a Name?

A good name is rather to be chosen than great riches,
and loving favour rather than silver and gold.
(Proverbs 22:1)

What is in a name? Your name identifies you and separates you from another person. What someone is called or labeled is arbitrary compared to their intrinsic qualities. One definition supplied by Freedictionary.com expresses that a person's name is the greatest connection to their own identity and individuality. It is the most important word in the world in each person's perspective.

In biblical times, many persons were named even before birth based on how pleasant or unpleasant the circumstances surrounding the family at the time. For example, *Adam*, the first man that was made; his name means Earth. *Yeshua*, which is one of Jesus' names means to deliver and to rescue.

There are also instances where God changed person's names to accommodate a definition to correctly identify who He desired them to be, for example, *Jacob* means to follow and to circumvent. But God later changed it from Jacob to *Israel*, which means one that struggled with divine Angels.

Simon the one who heard the Word of God was also changed to *Peter*, meaning a rock. The spiritual transformation from *Abram* which means exalted father to *Abraham*, means multitude. All these changes were made to facilitate God's purposes for His servants.

Oftentimes we are given names with negative connotation based on acts that we have committed in the past, and/or is still committing, 'whore', 'unfit mom', 'cheater', 'adulterer' or any other misfitting labels that society affix to our characters. We even sometimes start viewing ourselves according to these demeaning labels. However, no matter how devious we are, God views us differently. He can change the hearts of the vilest man.

Most times some people have a name change to identify who they now have become. They have renounced their old name and have taken on a new identity in Christ in the same manner that Saul changed his name to *Paul*.

We may not take on a new name here, but we can be assured that we will have a new name in Heaven. As a matter of fact, God already has the name plate that we will wear when we make that transition. Therefore, no matter what our past may look like or how we are deemed by others, we can rest in the assurance that God sees us as a new creation when we allow Him to transform us.

Prayer: God, I understand that I am a new creation. A brand-new man. Old things have passed way and now I am renewed. Give me the name that you want me to have, with the identity that you want me to possess. So that when others see me they can see you in me. Make me a reflection of you. In Jesus name. Amen.

Beauty, rise form the ashes and claim the new name your Heavenly Father has in store for you!

Day 6

What Anointing do you Operate Under?

But the anointing which ye have received of him abideth in you, and ye need not that any man teach you: but as the same anointing teacheth you of all things, and is truth, an is not a lie, and even as it hath taught you, ye shall abide in him. (1 John 2: 27)

When I prophecy to people, the Lord sometimes give me a name to associate with the individual to whom I am prophesying for them to have an understanding of who they really are. Sometimes the Lord says, "you operate under the Moses anointing", meaning that they possess similar virtues and personality to Moses. Or Esther, or Isaiah or Ezekiel among others.

Even for me, one day at church I felt the Holy Spirit moving through me. I started crying as per usual, and

I heard the Lord said "Jeremiah" and later I understood. I was spiritually operating under the Jeremiah anointing. It immediately dawned on me. Jeremiah was also called the weeping prophet hence me weeping under deep prophetic encounters.

I garnered an understanding of the prophet's characteristics and traits and analyzed them to see which ones I was more aligned in relation to Jeremiah in his calling and his walk with God. Jeremiah himself also suffered greatly for the Kingdom of God. He was hated by many, yet still he persisted in carrying out the works of the Lord.

Each time Jeremiah fell, he rose back up to deliver God's message and God protected him. Even in the most tumultuous time, he rose from the *ashes* over and over. Like Jeremiah, I have fallen many times and have risen from the ashes more beautiful than my last encounter.

We can also acquire different anointing in different seasons as we mature in Christ. Bible characters are a guidepost so we can identify where we are in God.

What Bible character virtues are you most associated with? I implore you to study such character as it is revealed to you by the Holy Spirit and derive the messages and lessons the Lord wants to teach you in the different seasons of life.

Child of God, you are anointed for an appointment. Take some time to listen to the Holy Spirit and allow Him to direct your path in your spiritual walk as you rise from the ashes and claim your beauty in Christ Jesus.

Pray: Lord thank you for your holy anointing. Thank you for anointing me for your purpose. I understand that my body is the temple of your Holy Spirit. You have equipped me for the call. Help me to understand as I try to establish your name, give me the faith, courage and boldness that I need to accomplish the task. Help me to abide in you. In Jesus Name. Amen

Beauty, rise from the ashes and claim and name the anointing on your life!

Day 7

It is Over for the Devil

Be sober, be vigilant; because your adversary, the devil,
as a roaring lion, walketh about, seeking whom he
may devour: (1 Peter 5:8)

S atan the enemy will try to usurp God's purpose for
your life with apocryphal stories like he did with
Eve in the Garden of Eden. He thrives on our misgiv-
ings, fears and disbelief in God. He clouds our judgment
and fills us with feelings of doubt, deception and defeat.
The Devil is an enemy of God. Therefore, he relishes in
the fact that we lose God's version of ourselves when we
give ear and yield to his beguiling allurements.

We are constantly blinded and devoured by him and this
makes it easy for us to forget our true authenticity. It is
therefore up to us to live by 1Peter 5:8. *Be alert and*
sober minded for your enemy the devil prowls around
like a roaring lion, seeking for whom he may devour.

Understand that the devil led a revolt against God and His sovereignty in Heaven and was cast out. He was privy to the splendor of Heaven, and now he is disgruntled and doing his absolute best to prevent us from reaching our full divine purpose and potential in God. As a matter of fact, the only way he can hurt God is by turning us away from Him. But in the end, God wins. God always win.

Stand firm in who you are. Know your God given identity. Romans 8:17 tells us that we are heirs of God and His kingdom. Do not let the devil cause you to lose your birthright. He is the defeated foe, and it is already over for him. So, rise from the ashes and know that you were bought with a price, you are God's masterpiece and once you have established your identity in Him, He will see you through.

I find this song by Jamaican gospel artist, Kukadoo very comforting and it is my prayer that it will also bring comfort to your heart:

If I am not living for Jesus, then I cannot be happy. I only live my life to please the Lord. I am working for a robe and a star in my crown. I only live my life to please the Lord.

Prayer: God, help me not to fall in the snares and traps of the devil. Help me to understand the power and au-

thority that I have over him; that no matter how cunning he is we are always able to win. May we find comfort in you our Savior. Help me to resist temptation and lead us in the paths if righteousness. In Jesus' name. Amen

Beauty, rise from the ashes and rejoice. It is over for the Devil!

Giftings

Gifting according to the Oxford Language Dictionary is to give something as a gift, especially formally or as a donation or bequest. To present someone with a gift or gifts. Endow with something.

Spiritual gifts are enablement or capacities that are divinely bestowed upon individuals.

For the next seven days we will be focusing on the theme of Giftings. When God raises us out of the ashes, He equips us so that we can fully exude His beauty.

Day 8

Knock Knock...Who is there?
Your calling.

But unto everyone of us is given grace according to the measure of the gift of Christ... And he gave some apostles; and some prophets; and some, evangelists; and some, pastors and teachers; (Ephesians 4:7&11)

Since I was a child, I have had some experiences that I would consider supernatural. I have seen angels and have had dreams of many things that came to pass in the exact order to include my grandmother's passing, accidents among other things that blew my mind. I had prayed for people who testified that they were healed. Deep down inside I have this strong urge of knowing and discerning things. I remember the Lord instructing me to attend Bible College, but I did not go. I do not know if I was simply scared of the possibilities or feared the change.

What is my life's purpose? What is my divine calling? Why was I born? are some questions that bombarded me daily. Sometimes we may feel lost, or sometimes we might have an inkling of what the answers are to these questions, but we are uncertain. One thing for sure is that whatever your calling is, whatever you are ordained to be, it is already in you.

You are not becoming, you are being. You possess the criteria that God has equipped you with.

Apostle Paul described calling as a summons from God to practice spiritual gifts such as teaching, preaching, prophesying. Our carnal gifting is usually an indication of our spiritual gifting and where we should use it. For example, I am a beautician (hairstylist, makeup artist), but I also discovered that I am a prophet. With my skills of being a hairstylist, I not only transform heads and hair, but I also transform hearts by sharing the heart of Christ with His people.

Your calling is within you waiting to be discovered and established. Open your soul for the out-pouring of the Spirit and allow God to instruct you on your life's mission.

Prayer: Lord I want to save souls for your Kingdom. Thank you for entrusting me with your gifts to serve others. Let me not lose sight of the mission. Provide me with the gift of discerning that I may share and edify the people with whom you desire. Use me as an instrument of thine. Thank you. In Jesus' name. Amen

Beauty, rise from the ashes and answer the calling on your life!

Day 9

The Gift of Anointing

But you have an anointing from the Holy One. And all
of you know the truth. (1 John 2:20 NIV)

When I answered the call as a prophet, I thought I had to seek out the finest and the best to teach me. Initially, I thought I was going insane with all the revelations that I was getting. I also had persons around me that were already pastors and apostles, and I started viewing myself as mediocre in comparison to them. I would scour the internet day and night to seek the most eloquent and most replicable in my field. I wanted to be profound.

One morning after the Lord instructed me to start my ministry, I felt immensely fearful and doubtful in my abilities. I was overcome by the thought of people ridiculing me and I just knew there would be harsh critics.

I heard the Lord reassuring me as He said, "I have already equipped you for this. The anointing is God's selection of you and then He pours the oil on you." It is so funny that I am writing this topic today as He also spoke to me yesterday on this same matter. He said the anointing is not for you to be free from the pressures of life, but the anointing is for you to endure the pressures of life.

God is so amazing, and He gives the best gifts. He wants to gift you with His sweet anointing. Walk in your calling and receive His precious anointing.

Prayer: God, thank you for choosing me. Most of all help me to wrap my mind around the fact that you chose me. Let me not get caught in doubt and fear but may I always remember that you gave me power and a sound mind. All I need to do is to open my mouth so that you can do your part and fill it with the right words. Help me to bring comfort to your people. May your Holy Spirit abide in me. In Jesus' name. Amen

Beauty, rise from the ashes and receive the sweet anointing of the Holy One!

Day 10

Gifts and Purpose Revealed

Great in counsel, and mighty in work; for thine eyes
are open upon all the ways of the sons of men: to give
everyone according to his ways, and according to the
fruit of his doings: (Jeremiah 32:19)

Your real purpose will be fully discovered in your spiritual gifting. This awakening will light the fire and illuminate your life's path and kindle the passion for you to fulfill your purpose. A few years ago, I recall the Lord speaking to me continuously for a whole week. I would wake up and hear Him speaking to me boldly. I remember, He said to me, "I will make you a fisher of men".

I was intrigued by the statement but disregarded it along with all the other dreams and visions that I had gotten, up to that point.

I recall being in two trances. In these trances, it seemed as if the Lord lifted me and showed me the earth from above. He showed me so many spiritual things. I was scared as I had never seen or heard anyone in my immediate circle or at the church I was attending at the time relating any such experiences.

I would go to places and meet people (complete strangers) and suddenly have this "knowing" about them. The Lord gave me the unction to go on a seven day fast. It was during this time that I realize that I was a prophet. The lord started speaking to me even more in depth; my visions, dreams and sensitivity to the Holy Spirit was amplified.

The Lord was instructing me on how to dress, how to fast, what scriptures to read and how to prophesy. I was scared but it was as if the Lord had a hold on my mind and nothing of my will was done. I became a robot for the Lord. Carrying out his wishes except for a few auto fahren mishaps.

Fear not! Whatever your gifting is, God already has your people lined up to hear from you. The Word declares that your gift will make room for you and take you in the presence of great men (Proverbs 18:16). Whatever your spiritual gifting is, whether you are an apostle or prophet, evangelist, pastor or teacher, God's calling is for the equipping of the saints for the work of your ministry. Your people, that is, those who are assigned to you, are ready and waiting for you.

Prayer: Dear God, sometimes I feel incpt; I feel as though I do not know what I am doing. I sometimes feel inadequate to deliver your Word. I sometimes feel unworthy of the mantle. But help me to understand that I am ordained, appointed and anointed by you. Let me walk with confidence knowing that you, my Father is with me. Prepare the hearts of the people that when you speak, it will take root and bring forth good fruit in their life. Thank you. In Jesus' name. Amen

Beauty, rise from the ashes and allow the Holy Spirit to reveal your gifts and purpose!

Day 11

Gifts Developed: Hone your Skills

For the Lord giveth wisdom; out of his most cometh knowledge and understanding. He layeth up sound wisdom for the righteous. He is a buckler to that them that walk uprightly. (Proverbs 2:6-7)

After accepting and embracing my calling, the Lord gave me somethings that He later revealed to be my spiritual tools; a blue flag, olive oil, frankincense and myrrh. He told me to make an altar, a secret place for quiet time with Him; where I can lay at His feet and be fortified by Him.

On April 21, 2021, I had a full blown Holy Spirit takeover. It was as if I was consumed by God himself. I was lying in bed and got the urge to listen to a particular song. I started singing and worshipping. I stood up and was just worshipping and that was it. The Holy Spirit came upon me in full force.

I started to speak as if I were being controlled. I was saying utterances of "Jerusalem and Israel, woe be unto them who lead my children astray" and something about a "reset" that will occur in the world. The Lord held me for 15 minutes, which seemed like forever. I was crying and prophesying things to come in the world (which has come to pass).

After the Holy Spirit released me, I called my husband who was at work and I told him to come home as I was scared. I felt very tired and thought I was going to die, and my husband just thought I was going crazy.

Since then, I have completed a course at a school for the prophets. I garnered a better understanding of my calling on how to operate in the prophetic. I have read many books as my gifts are being developed and matured. I am still learning, but I am better able to flow in the office of a prophet.

Initially, your calling (whatever it may be) might feel crazy and uncomfortable to you. It might seem surreal, but once you get in the flow and embrace the anointing, you will understand your true calling and your true purpose then you will develop and mature your gifts accordingly. The Holy Spirit will teach you.

Prayer: God, I thank you for your knowledge, wisdom and understanding. I believe that you will order my steps in the way I must go. Please show me you. Help me to study your Word write it upon my heart so that you may take me to higher heights and deeper depth in you. In Jesus' name. Amen

Beauty, rise from the ashes and allow the Holy Spirit to hone and develop your gifts!

Day 12

It is Your Season

To everything there is a season, and a time to every purpose under the heaven. (Ecclesiastics 3:1)

In every aspect of my spiritual journey, the Lord has given me dates and instructions to initiate my calling. He gave me a seven day fast. He told me to get baptized and that I was to go on a seven-day shut in fast as He was going to usher me into ministry as a preacher. I got baptized in October the 18th 2020 and began my fast immediately. During the fast, every morning I woke up preaching. God gave me inspired messages that I would rush to jot down. It was as if He was right beside me dictating what needs to be written.

The Lord told me to get into ministry. I was delaying the process. He instructed me to get a podium. I did not get the podium immediately. One day I was shopping online and buying new wardrobe pieces when I heard the Lord say, "You better not buy those and not purchase the podium". I bought the podium immediately. The podium was sitting at the salon for 2 months.

I had just returned from Jamaica. I went into the salon and the Holy Spirit took me over and I heard the Lord say, "It is time. It is time to share the gospel." I decided to start Bible Study as I was already doing mini services on Tuesday mornings. The date was set for February 3rd, however, I became ill with the corona virus and it was delayed during these two weeks.

I had just started a 21-days fasting. I was revisiting my prayer box at the altar in which I saw the note from back in October where the Lord told me that my ministry would start in February. My mind was blown. For every aspect of my calling, the Lord had already allocated a certain time.

When your steps are ordered by the Lord, you receive the most and best results. Pay keen attention to dates and times where He tells you to initiate or complete specific tasks.

My friends, it is your season to walk in the giftings the Lord has deposited in you. Surrender your all to Him and allow Him to use and establish you. God's way is the best way.

Prayer: God help me to understand your perfect timing. You said there is a season for everything under the Heavens. Let me understand when the time is right; not dictated by my emotions or ego but by my need to be in divine alignment with you. You are my Father, and you have orchestrated all things well. Therefore, develop my confidence and faith in you that even when others are in their season, I don't get jealous, I just wait on mine. I know you will be on time. Thank you for loving me. In Jesus' Name. Amen

Beauty, rise from the ashes and walk in your season!

Day 13

What is Your Mission?

Above all, love each other deeply, for love covers a
multitude of sins. (1 Peter 4:8 NIV)

Your personal mission defines the impact you want to have on this world and the overall purpose of your life. It is the core of who you are; the essence of your being.

I find that in the carnal world I have a deep desire to transform women. I use my talents as a hairstylist and makeup artist to do that. I instill self-esteem, self-worth and self confidence in my clients when they sit in my chair. They are not only beautified physically, but they are also lifted mentally and emotionally. Our conversations are uplifting and motivating. I sympathize and empathize with those who are experiencing burnout and I speak life over them.

I have always felt an urgent desire and passion to bring healing to the heart, specifically women's hearts. Now in my spiritual life as a prophet, I am able to do the same, but more effectively. I exalt edify and comfort the broken hearted as God leads me to.

My personal mission is seeking souls for the Kingdom by assisting in healing the hearts of others through Christ. I want to live a life that is worthwhile and leave behind a legacy; a legacy of love. And it is through my work I fully discovered my true purpose of being the mouthpiece of God to the broken hearts; helping others to rise from the ashes and walk in the beauty of holiness.

God desires the same from you. He wants you to hone and develop the gifts He has given and take up your mission to heal the hearts of others in whatever way you are able. Whatever He has given you to do, do it diligently and in love.

Prayer: God let me forever chase after you so that you can give me an infilling of you. With you fully in me, I will have nothing to give but you. You are the one who can fill every void in every capacity. You can heal our hearts and heal our wounds. I understand that where my treasure is there my heart will be and so I ask that you help me to find my legacy in you. In Jesus' name. Amen

Beauty, rise from the ashes and take up the mantle!

Day 14

Renouncing Self

Then Jesus said unto his disciples, if any man will come after me, let him deny himself, and take up his cross, and follow me. (Matthew 16:24)

Jesus flipped me like a burger. I associate this phrase with my experience based on the manner that the Lord transformed my life. One day I was having a jolly ole time with the devil, reveling in the pleasures of the world and the next moment I was flipped to full repentance and declaring the works of the Lord.

I remember the Lord told me to stop committing presumptuous sins. I did not care as I carried on as if my life was my own. The Lord rebuked me again in a sterner voice. He said, "Didn't I tell you to stop?!" And that was when I made a detour and committed to walking the straight and narrow.

The Lord had opened my eyes to the world and to the spiritual realm. I saw all the sinful things I was doing, and I was truly ashamed. Even though I thought I was living a good enough life, I considered myself a decent and productive human of society, I was crucifying Christ afresh daily and breaking my Savior's heart.

We are no longer our own, we have to follow God's will to be perfect in Him. God's will now supersedes our own. If you genuinely want to experience a renewed and fulfilling life in Christ, you must live the life that God, Our Father, desires for us. We must forget about ourselves and fully surrender to God and walk in the path that He created for us. He has the blueprints. God will not force a relationship with us, but he desires an intimate connection based on freewill.

Once we get to know Him and grasp His full grandeur, then we will choose the life that He has already planned for us. No need to put your thinking cap on and ponder over it; Jesus has it all planned out.

It may get difficult. You may get weary, you may become disheartened, but God will be there to help you carry the cross when you renounce self and dedicate to living a life in full consecration and submission to His will.

Prayer: God, please send me endurance and persever-
ance so that I may walk in a manner worthy of my call-
ing. I understand that there will be times when I will be
disheartened. In such a time, remind me to cast all my
cares on you. I want to live a life that is pleasing to
you. This task may not be easy as the devil will try his
utmost best to derail me. But God. please keep me an-
chored in you. Don't let me fall. Help me to yield not to
temptations; deliver me from evil for thine is Your
Kingdom, Your power and your glory. In Jesus' name.
Amen.

Beauty, renounce self and rise from the
ashes!

Worship

The feeling or expression of reference, an adoration for a deity. Worship is the acts or rights that make up a formal expression of reference to God.

For the next seven days, we will be focusing on the theme of Worship. I pray that at the end you will have a deeper understanding and appreciation for praise and worship.

Day 15

Praise is Taught, Worship is Sought

Yet a time is coming and has no come. When the true worshipers will worship the Father in Spirit and in truth, for they are the kind of worshippers the Father seeks. (John 4:23)

Praise stems from recognizing the acts of God. Worship comes from the core of the worshipper and what God means to them. It comes from the heart. Praise includes singing and dancing and lifting of hands in reverence to God.

When I worship, I do so as if I am in the presence of God, at His feet. When we worship, we should do so with the knowledge that we are in the presence of the King of kings, the Lord of lords, Elohim, Adonai and El Shadai. We should take on a different posture. We must adorn ourselves with reverence.

When we have the capacity to understand and acknowledge God's magnanimity, His sovereignty, we humble ourselves before Him; we surrender, we empty ourselves and make room for Him. When we come to the end of ourselves, we come to the beginning of Him.

God is calling for a deeper worship. No longer should we stay at the seashore and just get our feet wet. We need to come deeper into the ocean; to be fully submerged and surrounded by Him where we only depend on Him. God wants us to lose ourselves in Him. When we come into the full understanding of God, we give him that unbridled praise and a more meaningful worship.

My friends, you were born to worship. Your inner soul craves the presence of God. While your style of praise may be influenced by your church or the people you associate with, worship was imprinted on your heart from creation. Lift your soul and pour out the worship within. Shout a hallelujah for what God has done for you. Let the Spirit take over and have His way with you.

Prayer: God my Father, my Lord, my Savior. I ask you to come into my heart today. Come in and fill this room. Saturate me with your anointing. Give me a heart of worship; a heart that bows to you, a heart that's clean and pure. I give you all the glory. I give you all the praise. You alone are worthy Father. I want to be connected to you. I want to be encapsulated in you. I want every aspect of my being to be filled with you. Let your blood run through my veins. In Jesus' name. Amen

Beauty, rise from the ashes and worship your Creator!

Day 16

Fasting Feeds the Soul

When you fast do not look somber as the hypocrites do, for they disfigure their faces to show others they are fasting. Truly, I tell you, they have received their reward in full. But when you fast, put oil on your head and wash your face, so that it will not be obvious to others that you are fasting, but only to your father who is unseen; and your Father, who sees what is done in secret, will reward you. (Matthew 6:16-18)

I remember before my 21-day Daniel fast (that birthed this book), I was not sure that the Lord was urging me to initiate it. I did not know fully what the fasting process should entail. I did not know which of the fast to do and when to commence. However, everywhere I went, I would see the number 21. Every song I listened to had some message or connection to 21 and the books I read was suggestive of a 21 day Daniel fast. It was as if it was chasing me.

One night in my prayer room, it happened again, another "21" showed up. I asked God to send me a definite sign of which fast He wanted me to go on. "Please tell me clearly where there is no obscurity".

I began to research books on the Daniel Fast and bam! There it was; a review with my name on it. A mom had bought a book I was looking at for her daughter. She had gifted the book to her daughter as a surprise. And now she had come back to give a review and my name was on it. Coincidentally, her daughter's name was also Kerri. I was so excited, and the realization dawned on me meaningfully that God knows be me by name.

God wants us to deny ourselves of the world and its pleasures and feed our soul. When you fast from things of this world, you feed the soul. When you develop this type of intimate relationship with Him, He speaks to you clearly and amazing things are birthed. This book is a testament of that.

Fasting and prayer has been a proven spiritual mechanism to move the hands of heaven. It is like the protein or vitamin for the growth and nourishment of a Christian.

Prayer: God, I give my life to you. I exchange my will for your ways. Anoint me to surrender to you. Invest in my capabilities and teach me to fast as I should. I de-

sire to fast in a manner that pleases and worships you, but I lose sight and get sidetrack at times. Help me to not focus on dark clouds but let me see the silver lining. Let me remain steadfast on you so when I come out of it I may see your full glory and experience you deeper. I desire to be close to you God and if there are impediments in my way please remove and dismantle them, in Jesus' name. Amen.

Beauty, rise from the ashes and feed your soul with fasting and prayer!

Day 17

Erecting the Altar

Casting all your care upon him. For He careth for you.
1 Peter 5:7

The altar is the most sacred place. It is the place where we meet God. In the Bible, God instructed His children to erect altars and make sacrifices of thanksgiving, repentance and praise. I have been prostrated, stretched out, laid out at the altar and consumed by the Spirit.

I now understand why people go to the altar and even more why people should go to the altar. It is a different experience of worship when we go physically at Jesus' feet. Oftentimes we do not go to the altar because we do not see miracles performed there. Many do not see its significance or believe the power that emanates there. Because of this, we miss out on a burning bush experience like that of Moses when he was instructed to take off His shoes as he was standing on holy ground. Subsequently, we forfeit our healing, deliverance and our financial blessing.

I consider the altar at church, the VIP section. Our altars need not be a physical structure where we make an animal sacrifice to the Lord as in the days of old, but we make a sacrifice of submission within our hearts. The altar is the meeting place of God. Many biblical characters erected altars to God for different reasons.

The altar is a place of repentance, reformation, transformation, and worship. When we repent at the altar, we are really, sincerely, deeply regretful about our wrongdoings and sin. In repentance, we should cleanse ourselves and present our bodies as living sacrifice at the altar.

There is healing, love, obedience, forgiveness, happiness, strength, salvation, mercy, purpose, holiness, purity and everything good at the altar. This is the place where you leave all your cares; that is, fornication, unforgiveness, molestation, backbiting, fear, doubt, insecurity, sadness, disease strife, jealousy, gossiping, betrayal, hurting, envy and pride. An exchange takes place there.

We should seek to have an altar within our homes and wherever we find quiet time for God. This should be our meeting place. A way of reaching Heaven to welcome the presence of the Holy Spirit into our homes continuously.

Prayer: God, let me not be ashamed of you. Help me to seek you in times of destitution. I have no other friend like you and therefore help me to cling to your unchanging hands. I give to you the altar of my heart. I want to stay at the feet of Jesus continuously. I am not perfect by any means, but I know you will make me pure. My heart belongs to you. Deposit righteousness in me so that I can withdraw from the bank of salvation. God you are so sweet, and your mercy endures forever. May you reside in the altar of my heart, in Jesus' name. Amen.

Beauty, rise from the ashes and erect an altar of praise!

Day 18

You are Going to be Tested

*For I know that in me (that is, in my flesh,) dwelleth
no good thing: for to will is present with me; but how
to perform which is good I find not. (Romans 7:18)*

Once I was conducting Bible Study and sharing
with my audience how to crucify the flesh when
I was tested that very same day. I was also fasting, asking God to crucify the flesh. I was so distracted and
thrown off that I contemplated canceling Bible Study;
however, I decided not to give the Devil the victory.

Then one of the faithful listeners to my podcast called to
inquire if Bible Study would still be in session. I responded in the affirmative and considered the call as a
nod from my most wonderful Savior that I should proceed with the studies. During the session, I was sharing
snippets of a prophetic class I was enrolled in. We had
discussed Romans 7:18 where Paul speaks of the good

that we desire to do, we do not, and the bad that we desire to curtail, we do. It is embedded in us to.

My students began to share with me by confessing some of the spiritual undertaking they desire to do but fail. One related, "I try to read my Bible more, but instead I am distracted by Facebook and social media". Another added "I try to fast, I read my Bible but fasting is difficult. I cannot do it. I would go all day without food sometimes, but the day I decide to fast and pray is the day hunger gets the best of me".

Suddenly, the Lord told me to tell her that she needed to be on a three-day fasting. Funny enough, I just asked who would like to join and everyone was so excited about it. We decided to go on a three-day fasting together. They were all eager and ready for the undertaking.

While we decided and planned, the Lord placed it on my heart to buy them journals and pens to center them so we all could be unified. I consecrated the books as God instructed. He said blessings and favor were heading our way. How comforting.

The devil was trying to circumvent our blessings and our worship to God. But God won.

When we decide to serve God and do His will, testing and trials are inevitable. Satan will do his utmost best to discourage and throw you off course but hold fast and press through the ashes because there is beauty at the end of the tunnel of testing.

Prayer: God, I know you will deliver me from temptation because you have experienced it and will deliver me when I call on you. There are times when I might even fall but help me not to stay in sin. Help me to humble myself and ask for forgiveness. The race is not for the swift nor the battle for the strong but for those who endures. Help me to endure. Many times, I am ashamed, but you cast our sins as far as the East is from the West. Help me to comprehend your love for me. Help me to walk in your light. In Jesus' name. Amen.

Beauty, rise from the ashes and endure the honor of testing!

Day 19

Don't Treat Your Bible like Junk mail

Thy word is a lamp unto my feet, and a light unto my path. (Psalm 119:105)

All scripture is given by inspiration of God and is profitable for doctrine, for reproof, for correction, for instruction in righteousness: that the man of God may be perfect, throughly furnished unto all good works. (2 Timothy 3:16-17)

As I was closing Bible Study one day, I was telling my faithful audience that fasting prayer and reading the Bible brings us utterly close to God, in His tangible presence, where we can almost touch the anointing. One listener said to me "they aren't able to read the Bible as much as they desire." God whispered in my ears immediately and said they weren't opening His letter to them. They are treating the Bible like junk mail. This was so profound; the way he referred to it.

Many of us, if not all, receive junk Mail through the Postal Services or even in our email. Sometimes, if curious enough, we open. Just the sight or thought of it being unimportant, we toss it to the side as "junk mail" spam or garbage. We dispose of it immediately. Most do not even make it to the unopened mail pile. That is how God said we are treating the Word. This is sad news.

The Bible is a manual on how to live our lives. It is critical instructions on how to operate. It gives examples for us to understand the precepts and concepts of God, and if we are going to live for Him, we need to read the instructions on his prescription and follow the guidelines.

I implore you today, whatever you are going through, no matter how busy you are, open the Bible and start reading. A lot of people make excuses that they do not have time and that they do not know where to start. The truth is, we all make time for anything that is important to us. We need to condition ourselves to make God and His Word priority. Ask the Creator for direction and He will give you revelations. Just open the Word and feast on the goodness therein.

Are you happy that God's Word is likened to junk mail? So, what are you going to do about it? Are you going to toss and ignore His personal letters and love notes to the side or are you going to read them? My friend, let us no longer rob ourselves of the power that comes from reading the Word of God. Let's make His Word priority mail rather than junk mail.

Prayer: God, in your presence there is fullness of joy. Help me to stay in your Word daily. Help me to write the Word on my heart so that I will not sin against you. Help me to seek your guidance and approval in your Word. The Bible is the answer for all our problems we might have. However, it doesn't just bring answers in time of calamity, but it brings joy to our hearts.

I want to read your letters. Help me to open them and to eat your Word. Your Word is like comfort food to our soul. So delicious. May your Words continue to lighten my way and bring joy to my heart, in Jesus' name. Amen.

Beauty, rise from the ashes and read the Word of God!

Day 20

Rise and worship: Just Do It!

But be ye doers of the word, and not hearers only,
deceiving your own selves. (James 1:22)

I want to be an excellent Christian. I do not want to be mediocre. I do not want to be regular. I want to be exemplary. I want Christ to be in me. I want to embody the very presence of God. I want God to be proud of me. That is the type of Christ follower I aim to be. I want His DNA to be evident in my character. I want to be one who does not only talk the talk, but walk the walk.

This is the desire I have. And it sounds great, but am I willing to shed the extra baggage so God can mold me? Am I taking His letters seriously? Am I renouncing self so that God can fill me? Am I abiding by His precepts, laws and commandments? Am I ready to take up the cross and follow Him? Am I willing to destroy self to become *Ashes* so that God can make me over? Am I willing to be empty so that He can inhabit me? Am I willing to be the clay in the Potter's hand? Yes, I am. Worship is a lifestyle for me and it should be for you as well.

In order to be like Christ, we must ask God to make us like Him. Our daily prayer should therefore be, "Take my ashes and refine it and make me a figure of beauty reflecting Your glory".

Prayer: God, help me to apply your Word to my life. Help me to walk circumspect in your sight. May the world see my good works and glorify you, my father, in Heaven. Help me to be a true representative of you. The cross is heavy, but your yoke is easy and your burden is light. Let me not seek to carry the cross on my own but know that you are walking with me. This is nothing compared to the great reward of salvation and eternal life that we will receive if we remain true followers of Christ. Thank you for the opportunity to serve you and to reign with you in glory someday, in Jesus' name. Amen.

Beauty, rise from the ashes and worship: Just do it!

Day 21

The Blessings of Music in Worship

O come, let us sing unto the Lord: let us make a joyful noise to the rock of our salvation. (Psalms 95:1)

My lips shall greatly rejoice when I sing unto thee; and my soul which thou has redeemed. (Psalms 71:23)

One evening after Bible study, I was reading blessings and favors prayers to end my day on a good note. Numbers 6:24 was the 1st Scriptural prayer listed. I stopped and played the song "Blessings" by Kari Jobe and Cody Carnes. I remember this specific detail because earlier in the week one of my clients told me about this song. This was just like a confirmation as the Lord was bringing it to my knowledge.

The song fortified my soul. We were all aligned with the Word that the Lord had just given and all of us agreed to fast. The Lord gave me a vision of us being blessed. We were going to be rewarded bountifully for sacrifices that we were making. This is a gentle reminder that God really makes the best of every situation that rewards us greatly even when unseen and that He speaks to our hearts through songs.

On another occasion I was travelling to Atlanta for a hair show. The ride is 8 hours long, so I am accustomed to playing music as I journey. Instead of playing my regular Jamaican dancehall jams I was led to play nostalgic gospel songs from childhood. They were familiar and easy to remember; now that I am older, I have a better understanding of the lyrics and a deeper connection to the meaning and application of these songs.

I was playing a song from Glen Graham's album "Oh, if I missed Heaven; it would be better if I wasn't born. What would I say to God when I meet Him at the Judgment Throne? I would be so confused if I am refused from entering the promise land. For it is my only hope to live in the sweet Heaven." I was so deep into this song I started re-assessing my life and started crying.

I started worshipping and tears were flowing from my eyes. Then suddenly I had a vision Of God in Heaven sitting on a throne rocking out to the worship. It was huge. The place was massive and had no bounds. It was all in the color of bronze. He had a staff, and he was just rocking and shaking his feet. His attire was like that of a Roman soldier. His sandals were straps. I did not have a full look of his face, but I knew it was God sitting on the throne. I am certain He was rocking out to the song that I was playing while I was worshipping.

He was just worshipping with me, and I assume that He was excited at the fact that I was worshipping Him. Since that day, I have no option but to worship God and music plays a very important role in my worship.

I can't get enough of worshipping, singing and giving Him praise. After seeing God and His Majesty and His glory, there is no reason why I should turn back. There is feeling of turning back. There is no nothing else I can do but serve God and magnify His name and to be forever in his courts. God is amazing, and after having that vision there is nothing else that anyone can tell me about God's nonexistence, Hallelujah. It is over for the devil.

There is immense blessing in praising and worshiping God. Being able to sing praises to Him is one of the sweetest of life's pleasures and He connects with us when we press into His presence with a praise on our tongue and music on our lips. Music is the best way to usher in the Holy Spirit and when you are led by Him miraculous things happen.

Prayer. GOD, I thank you for your warm embrace and the music you have deposited in my soul. It gives me so much joy to know that I am in the palms of your hands. Put a song on my heart Lord so that I can worship you in the beauty of holiness. Please take my worship as an offering to you. I bow my heart to you. Cleanse it and make it pure. Lord I want to live a life that is pleasing to you and that will grant me access to heaven. I pray that you will let me see your glory. Reveal the things that I can see with the natural eyes to me so that I may have a better understanding of you, your Sovereignty. I am enamored by you. Please find me worthy in your sight. Grant me heavenly visions. In Jesus' Name. Amen

Beauty, rise from the ashes and sing great tidings of joy!

Epilogue

Worshipping with Angels

Thou wilt shew me the path of life: in His presence there is fullness of Joy; at thy right hand there are pleasures forevermore (Psalm 16:11)

I recall my first moment seeing Angels in Heaven while worshipping, and I was shocked. I was excited. They were worshipping and encouraging me to keep going. Of all these years of praise and worship I have never had such a Heavenly experience. This just shows that you must be in a deep worship, fully committed to God, giving up your heart to Him to break through the atmosphere.

Another day I got a glimpse of Heaven when I was having a good old bathroom shower revival that broke out into a deep worship session. The Holy Spirit was there in full effect. I dropped to my knees and started worshipping. Suddenly, I felt as if I was in a stadium with other people worshipping. As I was about to open my eyes, I got a view of Heaven yet again. It is like the Heavenly host was encouraging me to keep going and was happy that I was worshipping with such depth.

This type of worship does not come easy. However, God anointed me for worship. It is one of the best feelings in the world. There is nowhere else I would rather be but seek to cultivate an intimate relationship with Him and watch miracles, sign and wonders happen right before my eyes.

My friends, before my encounter with God I knew nothing of my Identity, Giftings or how to Worship. I was a broken vessel, empty and unfulfilled. I was in an ash-like state and then I came across the Lord of my salvation who has elevated me to heights untold. I do not share my experiences and encounters with the Holy one to brag and boast. I am merely showing you how He can lift you out of the ashes of your life, your circumstances and give adorn you with His beauty of Holiness.

Since I found my Jesus I am no longer just a Beautician for physical enhancement, but I now specialize in helping others discover their beauty in Christ.

My prayer is that you, beautiful one, will rise from the ashes as you establish your Identity in Christ, discover

your Giftings and Worship Him wholeheartedly and saturate yourself in His Glory.

I dedicate this prayer to you:

*God let me see your glory. I have heard of encounters
and testimonies, but Lord I want my own experience
with you. I pray that you help me to cultivate a gen-
uine, authentic relationship with you. God, I yearn for
your presence. Fill me with your Holy Spirit. There is
no one else I would rather have than you. Keep my
heart and my mind fixed on you. I desire a more intimate, meaningful communion with you, my Father.
Help me to stay aligned with you in my purpose and lift
me up from the ashes of my life and beautify me with
your glory. In Jesus' name. Amen.*

BEAUTY, RISE FROM THE ASHES

About the Author

Kerry hails from the beautiful island of Jamaica. She received an academic scholarship to the University of Charleston where she pursued a Bachelor of Business Degree.

Kerry has a deep love for all things God. A Beautician by profession, her life's mission is to help everyone she encounters find their true beauty in Christ.

Kerry had a divine encounter with God, and she has been radicalized by God for God. She describes her transformation as that from "Saul to Paul". It's from that encounter that this book was birthed.

She went to the School of Prophets at A.L.I.V. Ministries in North Carolina and has since been using her gifts to edify the Kingdom of God. She hosts Bible Studies at her Salon in Charleston and streams them weekly on her social media platforms. She is a philanthropist, a God-preneur and a true worshipper whose desire is to help others rise from the Ashes and exude God's Beauty.

Kerry is a big Jesus Gal!

Made in the USA
Middletown, DE
22 November 2021

52843304R00049